# THE DREAMERS ADVANTAGE

Including Real Dream, Vision, And Number Interpretations

Misha Wesley

Copyright © 2014 by **Misha Wesley**

All rights reserved. No part of this book may be used or reproduced by any means, graphic, electronic, or mechanical, including photocopying, recording, taping or by any information storage retrieval system without the written permission of the publisher except in the case of brief quotations embodied in critical articles and reviews.

**Misha Wesley/Rejoice Essential Publishing**

**PO BOX 512
Effingham, SC 29541**
www.republishing.org

Author's website: www.schoolofpropheticarts.org

Copyright © 2018 Misha Wesley

Unless otherwise indicated, Scripture is taken from the King James Version.

Scripture quotations marked (NLT) are taken from the Holy Bible, New Living Translation, copyright ©1996, 2004, 2015 by Tyndale House Foundation. Used by permission of Tyndale House Publishers, Inc., Carol Stream, Illinois 60188. All rights reserved.

Scripture quotations marked (ESV) are taken from the Holy Bible, English Standard Version. copyright © 2001 by Crossway, a publishing ministry of Good News Publishers.

All rights reserved.

**The Dreamers Advantage: Including Real Dream, Vision, And Number Interpretations/ Misha Wesley**

ISBN-10: 1-946756-26-1
ISBN-13: 978-1-946756-26-8
Library of Congress Control Number: 2018940617

Dedication

*This book is dedicated to every dreamer of every ethnicity. Your vision and dreams matter.*

—Prophetess Misha Wesley

# CONTENTS

INTRODUCTION TO DREAMS, NUMBERS, AND VISIONS......................................................1
INTRODUCTION TO THE REVELATORY REALM............................................................7
DREAM AND INTERPRETATIONS...................13
DREAMS/MEMORIES AND THE BRAIN.........22
SLEEP STAGES......................................................27
SLEEP PARALYSIS...............................................29
NUMBERS..............................................................32
TRIAD AFFECT.....................................................35
THE GEMATRIA....................................................58
ANATOMY OF DREAMS AND UNDERSTANDING GOD'S VOICE.................................68
DREAM DICTIONARY.........................................73

CHAPTER ONE

# INTRODUCTION TO DREAMS, NUMBERS, AND VISIONS

Dreams are something we all have, as individuals, adults, children as well as the entire Human race. However, the context and symbolism of the dream can sometimes leave the dreamer puzzled or even a bit confused. This often happens when the dreamer tries to reduce the dream to interpret its complexity with their natural mind. The problem some have with interpreting their own dream is that they digest the dream as a whole and interpret its meaning based off of emotions, feelings, actual life experiences, comparing and contrasting literal or natural symbols. Although dreaming is common, every dream contains an uncommon prophetic message for each particular dreamer in which God engraves the message on their hearts. It's hidden message contains a problem encoded with a spiritual solution for each and every circumstance that will; guide, direct, keep, warn, foresee, foretell, hold, unlock and counsel.

Dream in Hebrew is Chalam (pronounced: Khawlam) and means to be made strong; healthy[1]. The Greek Lexicon meaning of dream is Onar; ovap - meaning an uncertain derivation; to dream, in a dream[2]. So now we see here a deeper compelling comparison between these words as it is translated from English to Hebrew and Greek. Now let's take a look at the word "derivation" which means; obtaining or developing of something from a source or origin[3].

Therefore, it is a true statement that dreams can make us healthy and strong only if we know the derivation of its original source of the actual dream. Which brings me to dream sources and its origination. Dreams can be sorted into three different categories which then can be broken down further into sub-categories in which determine the actual summary of the dream. The three categories of dreams are:

1. Prophetic Dreams
2. Flesh Dreams
3. Dreams from the enemy

These categories are sub-divided as follows:

1. **Prophetic Dreams**: Calling dreams; warning dreams.
- **Calling dreams**: These dreams are usually filled with color, highly symbolic and the setting can be in unusual places.
- **Warning dreams**: These dreams will show you of an event that is taking place or about to take place. This would be God exposing something that is often hidden, dangerous, or potentially dangerous to you or those around you. God gives us these types of dreams because we sometimes cannot see what Satan is planning with our natural eyes. These dreams assist us in revealing the hidden snares of Satan.

2. **Dreams from the Enemy:** Fear Dreams; dreams that are dark in nature.
- The dreams from the enemy would be the dreams that do not line up with God's word. If the enemy seeks to steal, kill and destroy, John 10:10, then the dream realm would be no exception. Since we cannot be ignorant of Satan's devices, we must learn to arm ourselves. This means to cover ourselves with prayer and the blood of Jesus which protects

us even when the enemy tries to hit us with his best shot!

3. **Flesh dreams/Soulish, self-Conditioning**: The majority of these dreams come straight from our own mind, and our own emotions. These dreams that denote the condition of our heart and dreamer itself. Did you know that eating certain food before sleeping or taking certain medications can affect your dream life and how well you transition through sleep cycles?

The dream realm aids us to go into deeper realms of the spirit. If you are a dreamer, then you should be overjoyed because you have an advantage over the enemy to learn what he thinks you are not paying attention to. The dream realm helps us to go deep into the heart of God, into the deep realms of the spirit and search for the Lord's wisdom, power, and might.

Just like every dreamer won't be the same, every dream and vision won't be the same. A dreamer can dream of what I call a three-fold dream, in which contains different types of dreams rolled into one. Meaning one part can be prophetic, the other part can be fleshly, and another part can be a self-conditioning. The dreamer's spiritual state will determine the dreams length, category, and sub-category. You see dreams are not a one size fits all!

Dreams are never just "silly dreams", no matter how insignificant others or even you may think that dream is, it will always reveal your thought life, health, love life, heart, flesh, spiritual walk, people around you and their hidden motives. The deeper connected you are to the heart of God, the more secrets God will whisper and reveal to you in your dreams!

Not only will God reveal to us his secrets in dreams, but he will reveal them in visions and especially in numbers. Numbers are like a code, a combination lock to a safe and behind the combination lock, behind the door is a hidden treasure waiting to be found! I believe it was extremely necessary for me to write a section on dreams, visions, and numbers.

I have seen people try to interpret numbers. However, it bothered me because they were just scratching the surface of a topic in which God wants us to dig deeper on, and then expand upon it. Every single number interpretation I have done for anyone has been confirmed to be the truth by the person who first allowed me to interpret it. I don't believe that God gives dreams to us for us to simply dream. However, it's to ignite us, inspire us, warn us, direct us, and also, at times, free us!

Therefore, the gift of dream interpretation is not just a gift for me to hold onto and simply interpret dreams. However, it's to equip you to use your dreams to pray strategically over your regions, families, businesses, jobs, children, finances, and ministries. God actually combines visions, dreams, and numbers to actually unlock prayer strategies, divine plans and prophetic symbols and blueprints. Think of it this way, our lives are like one big literal puzzle and as we discover the "Jesus piece" we ultimately uncover a missing part of ourselves. Then we are not to just stop there, but to continue on. That "Jesus Piece" is only a doorway into all that he has for you! Remember this:

*It is the glory of God to conceal a thing: but the honor of kings is to search out a matter.*

*Proverbs 25:2*

CHAPTER TWO

# INTRODUCTION TO THE REVELATORY REALM

## THE WORD OF KNOWLEDGE:

This form of knowledge only comes from God. This knowledge is supernatural and know facts supernaturally. The gift of the Word of Knowledge refers to the ability to know facts about a situation or a spiritual principle that could not have been known by natural means. This allows someone to see a situation as God sees it. John 4:16-19 points to a perfect example of a Samaritan woman that comes to the well where Jesus was sitting to get water.

> *Jesus said to her, "Go, call your husband, and come here." The woman answered him, "I have no husband." Jesus said to her, "You are right in saying, 'I have no husband'; for you have had five husbands, and the one you now have is not your husband. What you have said is true." The woman said to him, "Sir, I perceive that you are a prophet.*
>
> *John 4:16-19 (ESV)*

This is an example of a Word of Knowledge. How else could have Jesus known this information without the woman telling him? It was by the Word of Knowledge that manifested by the spirit that was upon Jesus!

A word of knowledge can manifest by the spirit through a vision (mental picture; either opened eye or closed eye), hearing God's voice, or through a dream that the spirit of God has quickened to your spirit. The Word of Knowledge and understanding will *always work together*. Meaning, God will not give you a Word of Wisdom without giving you the understanding to know what that particular thing is. To interpret, means that you are able by the spirit, to explain or know something thoroughly. However, in order to know the meaning of a thing, you must first understand thing! That's why these gifts of the spirit function best together.

Depending on your operation and administration by the spirit, it will determine how often these gifts will manifest in your life. The office of the prophet will have these gifts in full manifestation more frequently and it will flow more strongly. However, each and every prophet *must be trained in this area of the spirit before this operation of administration can become fully functional.* No one is exempt from the process nor exempt from training by the means of tests, trials and errors. It happens, and that's why we have a father that overflows with grace!

## WISDOM APPLIED

Let's apply the word of Wisdom taken from Proverbs 8 (NLT) and gain a greater understanding of it.

1. Verse 1. Listen as Wisdom calls out! Hear as understanding raises her voice!
- Wisdom cries out for us to hear it's voice and to listen, open our ears towards the direction she calls.

2. Verse 2. On the hilltop along the road, she takes her stand at the crossroads.
- The crossroads symbolize the decisions that need to be made in our life. Wisdom stands

in the high place, with God, awaiting for us to answer her call before we make a decision.

3. Verses 3-8. By the gates at the entrance to the town, on the road leading in, she cries aloud, "I call to you, to all of you! I raise my voice to all people. You simple people, use good judgment. You foolish people, show some understanding. Listen to me! For I have important things to tell you. Everything I say is right, for I speak the truth and detest every kind of deception. There is nothing devious or crooked in it.

- If you carry God's true wisdom, then nothing devious should be hiding behind your decisions. You will not make crooked ones to manipulate another person or way. God's wisdom is pure, as well as the motives.

4. Verse 9. My words are plain to anyone with understanding, clear to those with knowledge.
- Here is the words wisdom and knowledge again. As you can see from the word of God, these gifts function in operation together.

5. Verse 12. I know where to discover knowledge and discernment.
- The definition of discernment is wisdom. The definition of wisdom in Hebrew means a

skill.[4] So, wisdom is a skill learned of a special kind of craft. To discern a thing is to have the wisdom of a thing. Discernment is not a judge of character, about a person, however, discernment is to know the motive of operation, intention, or an ability to obtain spiritual direction and understanding.

According to the Strong's Concordance, wisdom can be defined in various ways[5]. Wisdom (02451) (chokmah [word study] from the verb chakam - to be wise) is the ability to judge correctly and to follow the best course of action, based on knowledge and understanding. Wisdom is the ability to see something from God's viewpoint. Wisdom is "God's character in the many practical affairs of life."

Chokmah is the knowledge and the ability to make the right choices at the opportune time. The consistency of making the right choice is an indication of one's spiritual maturity. The prerequisite for this "wisdom" is the fear of the Lord. "Wisdom" is personified as crying out for disciples who will do everything to pursue her. The person who seeks chokmah diligently will receive understanding: and will benefit in life by walking with God (Gal 5:16).

Chokmah is used most often in Proverbs, so that the reader of the "wise sayings" might know wisdom and allow the Truth of God to govern his or her life. It follows that it behooves every child of God to meditate frequently and deeply on the Words of Wisdom.

# *Strong's Concordance*

***Chokmah:*** *Wisdom*
***Original Word:*** *חָכְמָה*
***Part of Speech:*** *Noun Feminine*
***Transliteration:*** *Chokmah*
***Phonetic Spelling****: (khok-maw')*
***Short Definition****: Wisdom*

\*\*Wisdom and understanding is comparable to having discernment\*\*

# *NAS Exhaustive Concordance*

***Word Origin***
*from chakam*
***Definition***
*wisdom*
***NASB Translation***
*skill (5), skill\* (1), wisdom (143), wisely (3), wits' (1).*

CHAPTER THREE

# DREAM AND INTERPRETATIONS

HERE ARE SOME DREAM AND VISION INTERPRETATIONS FROM REAL PEOPLE.

1.  **Example One**

Hi Misha, I saw how you interpreted some dreams. This prompted me to want to share a personal vision I received from God with you. On 5th December 2016, I was lying on my bed with my eyes closed but I wasn't asleep; I was very much conscious. Then I saw an American Starbucks coffee cup, but this time, it was a golden one. Then in front of the cup was written the word 'Aug' and suddenly it spelt out in full as 'August', this was written in black letters on the golden Starbucks cup I saw.

Then the vision lifted. Please, I would appreciate any interpretation the Holy Spirit gives you to me concerning what the vision means. Please note that Starbucks coffee is not sold here in Nigeria. I am looking forward to hearing from you soon. Thanks and God Bless. I am a Nigerian who has never been to America, nor tasted a Starbucks coffee before lol. I often hear about it and see it in movies and on the Internet.

### Interpretation One

Let me start by saying wonderful vision. The Interpretation is simple, however, quite detailed. Therefore, let me begin with the word "Aug" you saw that turned to August. The root God showed you is Latin and Greek meaning "increase" then as the word transitioned to August which is the 8th month, which is a month of new beginnings! According to the Jewish calendar, August is the 11th month, and 11 is the number of transition. But this month is called "AV". This month has great significance as it relates to where you've been and where you're going. AV is the month that means where your days of sorrow will turn joy. Isaiah 60:1 says, "to appoint unto them that mourn in Zion, to give them beauty for ashes, the oil of Joy for mourning...."

God showed you the Starbucks as it relates to a "longing" for. But this cup was golden, in scripture gold is popular, prized, wealth, "increase". God showed this to you because this was his plan for you. Starbucks is a very famous brand and has become a household name. Therefore, this will be a season of great popularity and increase for you. God is shifting you from mourning to joyful praises and songs. You will sing and dance as he catapults you to new heights and new dimensions in him. He is also making you a household name where all shall know your name. I keep hearing the word, "brand."

God is branding you in this hour right now because He's preparing you for that golden place. He is making your name great! Smile my dear, no more crying! I hear "fashion week." You'll be there. These are the promises of your heart and the promises of God for your life. God is making you a model for HIM. For The glory of Christ, do not divert off this path! Be blessed my dear. I also hear the Lord saying, " The blessing of the Lord makes a person rich, and he adds no sorrow with it." (Proverbs 10:22 NLT). "Get ready," says the Lord.

# EXAMPLE OF A WARNING DREAM

### 2. Example Two

I saw myself driving in many lanes like highways. In the back of the vehicle, a baby girl was crying. In the passenger side some dude that's in my church was teaching and telling me where to go. I don't know if you're familiar with the children's show "Reading Rainbow," but all of a sudden the church dude was sitting in a small steel chair. He had this big book. It was open on his lap and coming out of the pages was beams of bright rainbow colors. He seemed to be telling or trying to teach me something. This dream was not controlled by me and it happened so fast and felt so peaceful. I woke up and got ready for work, but it was the last dream I dreamt that day before work and it was so vivid. I want to know if it was a lustful and fleshy dream? Or from God or from the enemy and what does it mean?

### Interpretation Two

So here's the interpretation, right off the bat, I'll tell you that this dream was from God and He was actually "Warning you". Seeing yourself driving in many lanes or highways and a baby girl crying in the back of the vehicle, means several things. This part of the dream symbolizes the gift God has given to you. The baby crying, means you've forgotten about it and you've allowed those God-sized dreams to take a back seat. As I was reading over this dream, I heard the word "entrepreneur" or "vision". God has given you this massive dream or business idea to steward and you've actually been "misguided" regarding that. There are some voices in the church that you've allowed to speak into your life in reference to that and it has you "in the wrong lane." God is saying to stay in your lane.

Seeing some dude from your church in the passenger side, teaching and telling you where to go, him sitting in a small steel chair, with a big book in his lap and telling you something means you've allowed some voices in the church to speak into your life that have a "small position" in the spirit (hence the small chair/stool=small/tiny position). The fact that you were driving the car meant that you were in control the whole time. However, you allowed this guy to point you in the direction he wanted you to go, and that's why God said to stay in the lane I've placed you in! Don't be at peace with anyone dictating the direction your life is going besides the Holy Spirit. Get alone with God and seek Him. Seek Him for this vision, or entrepreneurial sized goal. I'm praying for you dreamer!

## 3. Example Three

I was inside a lobby, and I knew it was an architectural office. The office had architecture templates as displays in a table, and I was standing close to a door. I knew in my dream I was inside an office, inside another big building. I saw business people around; I was professionally dressed, but I don't recall the clothing. Suddenly this very beautiful young guy enters the office dressed in a cream suit color, and he had curly hair, and he was very sharp. That was my impression of him in the dream. I then saw myself walking with him, and during my walk, I saw that the floor was white marble, in front of a big glass window and lots of lighting. I also saw stairs going down, but my focus was in the big glass in front of me. I was holding a kid.

Suddenly, there was a big shake, and I saw him holding a small template with the same design of a glass roof, that broke. He said, I'm looking for the architect that will build a strong house for you, so when the shake comes you are safe. I don't recall anymore. I was thinking, is this dream referring to my faith or maybe a big shake its coming and the Lord is trying to put me in a safe place? I don't know and haven't really prayed about it. I think that guy was an angel, but again, I do need help to get the interpretation. Thank you, sister, in Christ.

## Interpretation Three

Hey woman of God! First of let me say this is definitely a calling dream. The Lord is calling you to your purpose. The Lord has called you to the mountain of business. Let's break this down so that you can clearly understand your calling/instructions from the lord. Seeing yourself inside a lobby, or an architectural office that had architecture templates as displays in a table means the following: The architectural scenery and templates represents that you are in a season of building. This is a season in which the Lord will give you the heavenly blueprints and instructions for how to build, design and where you should go. Seeing yourself standing close to a door mean that this door represented an access point in the spirit. The Lord says it's your door!

The man you saw was, in fact, an angel, and the awesome thing about angels is that he is assigned to give you the assignment. God has given his angels charge over you! Psalms 91:11. The angel has been assigned to help you design!! The Lord is giving you the blueprints to design a business for the business mountain. When you saw an office inside another big building, that part of your dream symbolized just this! For the marketplace, God has given you a unique and creative idea. And this shaking is a Spiritual Awakening!! The shaking will shake you to your very spiritual core! It's not a bad shaking, but a good shaking. Praise God!

Walking or running in your dream, symbolizes your faith (we walk by faith, not by sight [2 Corinthians 5:7]) and also your spiritual endurance, because Isaiah 40:31 says, "they shall walk and not faint." When you saw that the floor was white marble, and in-front a big glass window with lots of lighting, it symbolizes a heavenly place/ heavenly realm, hence the lighting, the marble floors. The glass windows represent the open revelations or visions God will show you concerning this creative business idea!

I love the part of the dream where you saw stairs going down, but you were focused on the big glass in front of you and holding a child. You weren't focused on the stairs which were going down, meaning "negativity" or "downfall" or "demotion." Your focus was on the revelation, the vision, or the big picture that God was showing you! Also, the child you were holding represents this creative idea the Lord has given, the gifts He's called you to care for and protect, amen! When you were holding a small template with the same designed of a glass roof that broke and the man spoke to you means an area in which you were hurt or weakened.

Your spiritual ceiling was shattered as a result and the Lord is rebuilding you stronger than you were before so that you may be able to withstand future attack.

*All the dreams that I have had the honor of interpreting, by the power of the Holy Spirit, has provided direction, correction, what is happening now and a prophetic word of what will come in the future.*

CHAPTER FOUR

# DREAMS/MEMORIES AND THE BRAIN

*"There are a hundred billion cells in the human brain all working together!"*

Visions are actually happening or what will actually happen (could be inner-eyes closed or eyes open-outer) Both of which contain a prophetic message. Let's take a look a look at a common issue when it comes to dreams, and that is the memory. Before the Lord allowed me to interpret dreams, I spent years in heavy research regarding dreams, the brain and the way it shares and stores memories. The brain's consolidation process is imperative when it comes to memories, dreams, and visions.

Consolidation is the processes of stabilizing a memory trace after the initial acquisition. It may perhaps be thought of part of the process of encoding or of storage, or it may be considered as a memory process in its own right. It is usually considered to consist of two specific processes, synaptic consolidation (which occurs within the first few hours after learning or encoding) and system consolidation (where hippocampus-dependent memories become independent of the hippocampus over a period of weeks to years)[6].

After consolidation, long-term memories are stored throughout the brain as groups of neurons that are primed to fire together in the same pattern that created the original experience and each component of a memory is stored in the brain area that initialized it (Example; groups of neurons in the visual cortex a sight and the neurons in the amygdala store the associated emotion). Indeed, they may be encoded redundantly, several times, in various parts of the cortex, so that, if one engram or memory trace, is wiped out, there are duplicates or alternative pathways, elsewhere through which the memory may still be retrieved.

In other words, our brains keep copies of memories. The brain stores the sight of the memory as well as the emotion, and therefore, it's possible to have one without the other. You can remember, the feeling or emotion of that memory if the actual picture of gets erased. This often times are seen in a traumatic situation or events or someone that suffered traumatic brain injuries. Let's look at a scripture that I believe is critical in relation to this research.

*Don't copy the behavior and customs of this world, but let God transform you into a new person by changing the way you think. Then you will learn to know God's will for you, which is pleasing and perfect.*

*Romans 12:2 (NLT)*

Our minds must be transformed by the renewal of our minds in the word of God. We have to embed the truths of the word into our daily lives because the creator of our brain's neurological pathways knew that life would bring trauma, fears, worries, and defeat. However, the word of God transforms our thinking thus enabling us to see and discern his will which is "good, acceptable and perfect". How can we know what the will of God is if we are not reading and studying the scriptures?

This scripture is also true as believers go through deliverance. Whenever we go through deliverance, demons are cast out of our soul, which is the mind/

brain/will and the emotions. Emotions are stored in the amygdala. We need to retrain our brains to think as God thinks and to discern what is the will of God. You see, after deliverance, we are swept clean and become empty vessels waiting to be filled with the word of God. Luke 11:24 NLT, explains very clearly, when an evil spirit leaves a person, it goes into the desert searching for rest. But when it finds none, it says I will return to the person I came from. When it arrives, it finds the house swept clean and put in order". Please note that the Bible references symbolically that we are a "house". That's why when we dream about houses it represents, "us!"

This scripture denotes that after deliverance, our vessel is swept clean. Therefore, we need the word of God, or else we become in even worse condition than we previously began. Which leads me to Ephesians 4:23 (NLT): Instead, let the Spirit renew your thoughts and attitudes.

Our memories must be actively reconstructed from the elements scattered throughout the brain by the encoding processes. Memory storage is an ongoing process of reclassification resulting from the continuous changes in our own neural pathways.[6]

The realm of dreams, visions, and numbers are much heavier than just a mere interpretation.

However, it is imperative that we understand the mind/brain, and the nature of our own being and also that our "mind is renewed in the word of God." Otherwise, we would travel into illegal realms God has not allowed us access!

CHAPTER FIVE

# SLEEP STAGES

**SWS (Known as SLOW WAVE SLEEP)**

Bursts of neurological chatter take place during this phase of sleep. However, during this phase, is a period of deep dreamless sleep. It turns out that during this Slow-Wave sleep, there are these episodes where a lot of the cells in the hippocampus will all fire very close to the same time, says Wierzynski.[6]

**REM SLEEP (Rapid Eye Movement)**

According to the California Institute of Technology, REM Sleep is the phase in which dreaming occurs. The previously chatty neuron pairs seemed to talk right past each other, firing at the same rates as before but no longer in concert. The timing relationship almost completely went away during REM SLEEP.[7] Memories aren't consolidated during this phase of sleep according to the thousands of neurological studies. This research brings us to the following scriptures:

*For God speaks again and again, though people do not recognize it. He speaks in dreams, in visions of the night, when deep sleep falls on people as they lie in their beds. He whispers in their ears and terrifies them with warnings. He makes them turn from doing wrong, he keeps them from pride.*

*Job 33:14-17 (NLT)*

*Dreams are God's business (Genesis 40:8).*

CHAPTER SIX

# SLEEP PARALYSIS

What is sleep paralysis? Sleep paralysis is a feeling of being conscious but unable to move. It occurs when a person passes between stages of wakefulness and sleep. During these transitions, you may be unable to move or speak for a few seconds up to a few minutes. Every person that sleeps, passes about 5 phases of sleep per sleep cycle. As we go through these stages of sleep, our body must be able to come out of it. Sleep paralysis occurs when the body has trouble making these transitions. Let's look at two different types of sleep paralysis: Hypnagogic sleep paralysis (predormital), and Hypnopompic (postdormital).[8]

1. **Hypnagogic Sleep Paralysis:** Happens when you're falling asleep.
2. **Hypnopompic Sleep Paralysis:** Occurs during waking.

Scientists have also concluded that this is more common among young adults and people with a history of mental illness. A Penn State study found the highest prevalence rates were in students and psychiatric patients. Research has consistently shown that the less sleep you get, the more exhausted you are, therefore the more likely you are to experience sleep paralysis and other sleep disorders. Furthermore, this is a sign that your body is not moving properly through the stages of sleep.

Mental Illness is a terminology that refers to a wide range of mental health conditions that affect your mood, thinking, and behavior. A specific kind of mental illness many people unknowingly suffer from would be Schizophrenia. The term is derived from the Greek words skhizein and phren.[9] Skhizein means "to split" and phren means, "mind." Which is a breakdown in the relation between thought, emotion, and behavior leading to a faulty perception, withdrawal, and mental fragmentation.

The bible speaks about double-mindedness which is an unstable mind, inappropriate actions or feelings, and disturbances in thought. According to Merriam-Webster, schizophrenia is a disorder of the mind[10], and the Bible states very clearly that a double-minded man is unstable in all his ways (James 1:8).

This is why the scriptures continuously speak about our Minds needing to be renewed in the word of God. God knew what he was doing when He said that and He said it for our own literal health! That's why it is so very imperative for even our minds to be submitted to God and our very thought life needs to be concentrated on things that are noble, whatever is right, whatever is pure, whatever is lovely, and whatever is admirable (Philippians 4:8).

CHAPTER SEVEN

# NUMBERS

Numbers have such a profound meaning to our lives than many believers fail to realize or acknowledge. Many people are not awakened to this particular realm of the spirit and how number interpretation can impact a prophetic message to a believer. Often times, numbers are codes, hidden within a specific message waiting to be unlocked. Like dreams, the realm of interpreting numbers is shared within the revelatory realm of information stated in 1 Corinthians 12:8.

The bible clearly states there are diversities of operations, but it is the same God that worketh all in all (1 Cor 12:6 KJV) This means that it is by the spirit who gives us the diversities of gifting's, but it is one God that does it all. The spirit allows the manifestation of that particular gifting to operate so that the body of Christ can prosper. You see, here in scripture, it clearly states, that the revelatory realm of the spirit is given so that we may benefit. Let's look at the operation of the revelatory realm and how it manifests. In 1 Cor 12:8, it says, "For one is given by the spirit the word of wisdom; to another the word of knowledge by the same spirit". Although the spirit will allow these two operations to work by itself or stand on its own through any believer he chooses, the word of wisdom and the word of knowledge works together to open up the realm of revelation.

This realm is meant to unlock, decode, breakdown, reveal, expose and unveil the very messages the Lord is saying to you, for your church, for your region or for your nation. I also want to make very clear the working of the gift of prophecy in connection to these two spiritual gifts. (1 Cor 12:10 KJV) Therefore, if you can access this realm of the spirit, you would have a heavy ability, by the spirit of course, of three gifts manifesting and working together all at once for the good or profit of whoever is receiving ministry.

I have interpreted countless of numbers for people that didn't give me any information beforehand, but the numbers they were seeing. Often times, I've never seen these people or never met them. However, it is the spirit of God who knows every hair on their head. It is God who knows even when they sit down or stand up. The Lord knows your thoughts even when you're far away. The Lord knows everything you do. The Bible says that such knowledge is too wonderful for us, and too great to understand. We can never escape the Lord's spirit! (Psalm 139:1-6)

CHAPTER EIGHT

# TRIAD AFFECT

Many people in the body of Christ have only scratched the surface of number interpretation. Meaning their information is limited and do not know how to properly minister to someone through number interpretation. Repeating numbers or seeing multiples of the same numbers, only means that the single meaning of that number has tripled in meaning and now takes upon a heavier, weighty spiritual significance. This is known as the **Triad affect.** Often times, people will see groups or three pairs of the same numbers in a row. For example; 333, 111, 222, 444, 555, 777, 888, 10.10, 12.12, 11.11, etc.

The **Triad affect** is a group or set of three connected numbers, it also denotes that it will affect 3 areas of your life.

# 111 (SEEING MULTIPLES OF THIS NUMBER)

I believe this number holds a heavy spiritual significance to our personal lives and in our world around us. This teaching wouldn't be right if I didn't begin with Genesis 1:1-5.

*In the beginning God created the heavens and the earth. The earth was formless and empty, and darkness covered the deep waters. And the Spirit of God was hovering over the surface of the waters. Then God said, "Let there be light," and there was light. And God saw that the light was good. Then he separated the light from the darkness. God called the light "day" and the darkness "night." And evening passed and morning came, marking the first day.*

*Genesis 1:1-5 (NLT)*

The number 111 speaks about setting and commanding things into order, into alignment, shifting things into place. God is commanding order and calling the light to shine through you. Prophetic message: I can't help but to see the valley of the dry bones in Ezekiel 37. I hear the spirit of the Lord say, "I am commanding dry bones to be refreshed!"

The apostolic mandate draws you to himself (Christ). It separates you from the world. This number also signifies the new beginning, a fresh start in 3 areas of your life. It denotes a new beginning and a fresh start because of what God did in the book of Genesis. He created, He commanded the world, separating the light from the dark. So, in our lives, the Lord God, separates his truth from the false, separating the chaff from the wheat, his word divides joint and marrow, soul and spirit! The number 1 also signifies unity.

*There is One Lord, one faith, one baptism. One God and father of all, who is over all, in all, and living through all.*

*Ephesians 4:5-6 (NLT)*

## 222 (SEEING MULTIPLES OF THIS NUMBER)

By itself, this number represents either:

1. union
2. division

3. witnessing
4. multiplication
5. verification/confirmation;

You definitely want to keep in mind that when you are seeing this number, the Holy Spirit wants to confirm a message that He has told you of what will soon take place or has taken place. However, whenever the number is seen in a series like this, it can mean a combination of all these things.

Genesis 1:6-7 (NLT) says, "Then God said, "Let there be a space between the waters, to separate the waters of the heavens from the waters of the earth." and that is what happened. God made this space to separate the waters of the earth from the waters of the heavens."

**Witnessing.** 2 Cor. 13:1 says, "This is the third time I am coming to you. In the mouth of two or three witnesses shall every word be established." I've noticed in the scriptures, there were always two traveling together in pairs, by twos doing missionary work, God's work, speaking and often preaching together.
- Paul and Silas;
- Barnabas and James;
- Paul and Barnabas;
- Junia and Andronicus;

- Elijah and Elisha;
- Adam and Eve;
- Husband and wife=Union

Luke 10:1 states that Jesus sent out the apostles by 2's. The bible even states that two are better than one (Ecclesiastes 4:9).

# 333 (SEEING MULTIPLES OF THIS NUMBER)

1. God calling your attention to a particular area.
2. God calls Samuel 3 times. It took three times to get his attention. (1 Samuel 3:4-1).
3. This is the third time I am coming to you (2 Cor 13:1).
4. Paul preaches in the synagogues for three months and argues persuasively about the kingdom of God (Acts 19:8).

This number also represents Christ. The scriptures reveal that this number symbolizes vegetation, seed-bearing fruit- meaning that you are carrying around something that can be given to someone else; as in a spiritual birthing that can take place. These-seeds will then produce the kinds of plants and trees from which they came (Genesis 1:11).

## **3 Also Represents The Spirit of Christ Being Released**

Mark 15:25 (NLT) says, "It was nine o'clock in the morning when they crucified him." From the 6am-9am=3 hours. 7=1, 8=2, 9=3. Jesus was crucified on the cross in the 3rd hour according to the amplified version or translation of scripture (9am).

The spirit of Christ was released in Mark 15:37 because he gave his last breath. Jesus rose on the third day. 3 also represents the resurrection; this emphasis is on the Power of the God's Spirit that was released into the earth to raise Christ from the dead because Christ was in the earth!

That's why it is so imperative to pay close attention to what God is saying, especially concerning the Triad affects. I have heard some people saying that numbers or seeing triple numbers are non-sense or the use of interpreting numbers are not necessary. I must disagree. The Lord speaks in so many different ways through his creation as he chooses, but only if we be open to his various avenues of speaking. What we must understand is that the lord will go to great lengths to get our attention. However, if we are not awakened to this, we will miss the very message, or call the Lord is conveying. We cannot close our selves off to his glory and say the avenues of which he speaks are non-sense because of ignorance.

## 444 (SEEING MULTIPLES OF THIS NUMBER)

444 denotes creative works; the number of creation; God completed the material universe on the 4th day. He brought into existence our sun, moon, and all the stars. Their purpose was not only to give off light but also, to divide the day from the night, thus becoming a basic demarcation of time. In essence, the number 4 equates to the world around us, the earth, the seasons and times. The anointing of Issachar as it relates to knowing what season the body of Christ is in, even for your own life. The Hebrew word for seasons is Moed[11], which is literally translated to mean 'appointed times' (divine appointments).

In Ezekiel 1:5, we notice four cherubims are introduced as living beings that looked human. I will break this creature down in another chapter. However, I will state that these cherubims are symbolic for the earth, and movement throughout the earth. Also, they represent, the dominions and rulership of those upon the earth and the four corners of the earth.

Acts 12:4 (NLT) says, "Then he imprisoned him, placing him under the guard of **FOUR** squads of soldiers each." This also gives the point of reference to **being covered on every side** like the four corners of the earth.

The four witnesses of God on earth are miracles, signs, wonders, and the gifts of the Holy Spirit (see Hebrews 2:4). Therefore, the number 4 is speaking to us concerning times and seasons for specific movements to come in the earth. God's spirit performing signs, wonders, and miracles covering the earth and the movement throughout it as the gospel is preached.

## 555 (SEEING MULTIPLES OF THIS NUMBER)

This number by itself is said to mean "Grace". According to Genesis 1:22, on the 5th day God says, be fruitful and multiply let the fish fill the seas and let the birds multiply on the earth. This verse is key because not only does this number mean grace, however, it's associated with multiplication. Let's further explore the reason of the five being multiplied.

In Matthew 14:13-21 we notice that Jesus feeds the five thousand. A closer look reveals the instruction Jesus gave to his disciples; Jesus replied, "They do not need to go away. You give them something to eat." "We have here only five loaves of bread and two fish," they answered. This denotes that the number 2 also is associated with multiplication. Then it goes on to say, Jesus took the five loaves and two fish, looked up toward heaven, and blessed them. What happened in these verses, is called a 'Prophetic act'. Jesus performed an act of provision, which would have a powerful manifestation in the nature of gaining supernatural provision.

Praying over your finances or food is not just something you do, but it means you are partnering with the Father to provide more of what you have by allowing him to multiply it two times over. Therefore, five is the number of Grace, provision, and multiplication. Can I take this just a bit further? Why am I asking? You know I will!

This number is also associated with God's glory and His anointing oil. God's glory is found in Exodus 26-27 as it describes the tabernacle in the wilderness. God instructs the Israelites in In Exodus 25:8, "make a sanctuary for me, and I will dwell among them". When God's presence shows up, it appears as a glory cloud. Within God's glory cloud are healings, signs, wonders, and miracles. In Exodus 30:23-25 we see the ingredients for the Holy anointing oil. The ingredients were directly given by God and contained five ingredients which are myrrh, sweet cinnamon, sweet calamus, and cassia.

## 777 (SEEING MULTIPLES OF THIS NUMBER )

The number 7 by itself denotes the hallmark of the Holy Spirits work. The number 7 has 7 symbolic meanings in scripture.

1. Completeness: Philippians 1:6 being confident of this, that he who began a good work in you will carry it on to completion
2. Fullness
3. Perfection
4. To swear
5. To Vow
6. To make an oath.
- Jacob bowed 7 times to the ground when he saw his brother Esau (Gen 33). This signified an oath and vow he made to his brother Esau.
7. It also means rest since the earth was completed on the 7th day.

As you can see, this number by itself is very simple to interpret, however, when it relates to a triad of the numbers 777 it could be any combination of these symbolic meanings. However, it would depend greatly upon the individual and the message the Holy Spirit speaks to you in regards to the prophetic ministry through that number.

Here is an example of a number interpretation request I received from someone regarding the number 7.

*"Blessings to you WOG. I'm growing in the spirit with God, seeking His face day by day, and fighting the flesh with the Holy Spirit. However, I always encountered the number 7. I was the 7th person to walk across the stage during graduation in 2015. I did a scratch off that is attached and 777 were on there as well. I just took a test for the postal service. My results were 77.7. I look forward to chatting or speaking with you."*

## **Interpretation:**

Hello Man of God! Wow, as soon as I read this, the Lord instantly spoke to me regarding what you wrote to me, and this is what the Lord says, "Since birth, I've marked you. Marked you for greatness to pursue the destiny, I the Lord has placed in your heart. I am perfecting you and perfecting the areas of your life, business, finances, and ministry. I've called you to the marketplace in business to spread the Gospel in various places and to people who do not know me. My perfection is upon you my son. I am daily loading you with benefits as you draw unto me in prayer and as you abide in me in the secret place. I am abiding in you. My son, I am blessing the work of your hands so that you may fulfill every good work I send you to." The Lord also showed me that you are getting and will be working for the postal service so your career there will be steady. Abundant Blessings!

### **His Response:**

"Glory to God! How accurate!!! I knew it! Yes! Hallelujah. I shout for Joy. Thank you, Lord God. My mom gave me up to God when I was first born. I'm being patience and allowing God to abide in me. God bless you, WOG".

In this example above of a real number interpretation, you see the fluidness of the gift of prophecy, word of knowledge and the word of wisdom working together to provide a clear and accurate message straight from the Father's heart.

## 888 (SEEING MULTIPLES OF THIS NUMBER)

The number eight has a basic significance even when tripled that has deep spiritual, biblical roots dating back to the book of Genesis. Abraham the father of faith had eight sons which symbolized a new beginning in the earth. Jesus appeared to his disciples eight times after He was resurrected and brought to life. The new eight also signifies the mark of the covenant.

*You must cut off the flesh of your foreskin as a sign of the covenant between me and you. From generation to generation, every male child must be circumcised on the eighth day after his birth. This applies not only to members of your family but also to the servants born in your household and the foreign-born servants whom you have purchased.*

*(Genesis 17:11-12 NLT)*

I have noticed an increasing amount of people in the body of Christ seeing the numbers 611, 411, 711, 911 and this is what it means: these numbers relate to the deeper revelatory realm of information, insight, spiritual wisdom, knowledge, and spiritual awakening to the revelatory. God is drawing you deeper into this realm because He desires for you to have a new level of spiritual maturity in this particular area. God's desire is to bring the operation of the word of wisdom, word of Knowledge, discerning of spirits and prophecy to full operation and allow them to flow together.

737- Boeing 737; powerful jet plane; ignitor of souls and hearts, separator of joints and marrow; power of the spirit; carrying the spirit of the lord with authority and reverence.

# 999 (SEEING MULTIPLES OF THIS NUMBER)

This number by itself signifies the fruit of the spirit and divine completion from the father. This number has three significant meanings in scripture:

1. The 9 gifts of the spirit
2. Sevenfold spirit
3. The 9 fruits of the spirit

Those who are particularly seeing the number 999 needs to know this is also in Strong's Concordance.

*999=Binah*

**Binah:** *An understanding*

**Phonetic Spelling:** *Bee-Naw*

**Word of Origin:** *Aramaic corresponding to Binah*

Daniel 2:21-22 says, "He changes times and seasons; he deposes kings and raises up others. He gives wisdom to the **wise** and **knowledge** to the discerning. **He reveals deep and hidden things**; he knows what lies in darkness, and light dwells with him."

999 in Hebrew, is Biynah, which means knowledge. This was Daniel's prayer as he interpreted the dream of the King Nebuchadnezzar. Daniel inquired

of the Lord. God opened up the realm of revelation and poured it over Daniel.

## THE FORMULATION OF A PROPHETIC WORD FOR 2018 THROUGH ONLY THE NUMBERS 4, 2, AND 12

### Interpretation of the Number 4

In the book of Ezekiel, beginning in 1 verse 3, notice that he was among the captives, by the Kebar River. In Hebrew, the word Kebar means to 'intertwine'. Ezekiel was not just among the captives, but he lived as they lived, intertwined, sharing in their suffering, but we notice he also sat beside a river. The river symbolized the spirit of God because it also says that the heavens were opened. So despite Ezekiel's captivity, the Lord still will reveals himself.

Let's further example the number four in chapter one of Ezekiel.

- Four living beings that looked human (Ezekiel 1:5).
- Under each of their four wings I could see human hands. So each of the four beings had four faces and four wings (Ezekiel 1:8).
- The wings of each living being touched the wings of the beings beside it. Each one moved straight

forward in any direction without turning around (Ezekiel 1:9). This represents the four corners of the earth. The earth touches every part of itself that it's connected to. "As the waters cover the sea" (Habakkuk 2:14).
- Each had a human face in the front, the face of a lion on the right side, the face of an ox on the left side, and the face of an eagle at the back (Ezekiel 1:10). The faces represented the faces of God's creation, dominion, and rule. The faces of the Ox, Eagle, lion, and human.
- They went in whatever direction the spirit chose, and they moved straight forward in any direction without turning around (Ezekiel 1:12). The living creatures didn't need to turn because they faced all the directions and they moved as the spirit chose. The spirit of God chooses where you go, he directs your steps, orders your feet, and provides the instruction. Pay close attention to the Cherubim that didn't need to think about where they went, they just WENT.

## Interpretation of the number 12

*12.12 Perfect Foundation of Governmental Order/ Governmental Perfection (Apostle)*

The number twelve when it stands on its own may mean God's perfect foundation of governmental order of perfection. On its own, this number symbolizes the twelve apostles that were a witness to the life and death of Christ. However, when this number is doubled, it takes upon a more hefty spiritual significance.

When a number is doubled, it takes upon the meaning of "2", which means witnessing. Why witnessing? Because in Luke 10:1 Jesus sent out the seventy apostles by 2's. The prophetic action that Jesus took in this scripture symbolizes the sending out and sending forth. The reason twelve is an apostolic representation of God's kingdom is because it represents the model of Christ and what he has commissioned; the sending and releasing of Gods people into every place throughout the earth to do the work of the kingdom.

The meaning doubles because we add the numbers up to equal an even more perfect number which is twenty-four. Twenty-four means the royal priesthood. In 1 Chronicles 23-24 David appointed 24,000. He supervised their work. David divided this group of priests and Levites. Also, in Psalm 72 describes how Christ, is a high priest and describes twenty-four ways of his rule. So let's combine what God showed me with 4, 12, 2.

CHAPTER NINE

# APOSTOLIC REFORMATION

In 2017, I released a video of how we will see the apostolic reformation. Shortly, after I released this word, many prophets and apostles came forth and revealed a similar message. Therefore, I want to combine these numbers to reveal God's message.

**1. Apostolic Age of Reformation.**

To reform means to make changes to something with the intention of setting it back on the right path. God is making changes now to the DNA of the Apostles and Prophets who are pure, prophetic, and peculiar. We will be seeing a rising of apostolic teachers of the fivefold and Apostles with a strong teaching dimension. Apostolic theologians will bring clarity and understanding to the scripture, who will stand as Paul stood with power and demonstration of the spirit, preaching persuasively to win souls for the kingdom of God.

## 2. Apostolic Teams

I see teams being sent out 2 by 2, witnessing the gospel to others in various regions and territories. Teams of 2 organizing and managing. You will witness a Rise of Apostolic Hubs, Businesses And kingdom assignments. This is an era in which denotes a time of maturity in the body of Christ. This is not a time to be weak or crippled by fear. However, it's a time to know your identity in Christ Jesus. I see new levels of organization and management coming to the Ecclesia where there was confusion and chaos.

This is a result of the rising teachers, apostolic theologians, kingdom businesses and hubs. There will be much equipping in 2018 for the Ecclesia. From 2018 and on, you'll see an increase of prophets and apostles in business dominating the entrepreneurial game; prophets who are masters in ecommerce, trading, and stocks. Organizational prophets and apostles obtaining high positions in secular companies reigning as Daniel reigned in King Nebuchadnezzar's royal court and the Spirit of the Lord will be heavily upon them. Don't despise working in a secular market or working among unbelievers in this era because the Spirit of the Lord will be with you as you release the light of Christ. Ordinary Churches operating without the spirit of God will die out quickly in this era, and the pastoral model will crumble if it's not led by a pastor that carries "apostolic DNA".

## 3. Age of the Apostles or Acts of the Apostles

I love how the book of Acts opens, making reference of how close the apostles were to Christ. After his death, he appeared to them on numerous times. He proved to them in many ways that he was actually alive (Acts 1 verse 3). In Acts 2, you see and read that the Holy Spirit came suddenly and there was a sound from heaven like a roaring of a mighty windstorm and it filled the house where they were sitting (Acts 2:2). God has shown me how He will drench His holy apostles and prophets in this new era and the power of the Spirit of the living God will be upon their lives so heavy.

I remember as I slept one night, I had a dream and in this dream, I saw Jesus commissioning a small group of apostles. He was preparing them to be sent out, and before He sent them out, He gave them a book to read from. It was an oath taken from the Gospel of Matthew 10:16 that these Apostles took. I remember looking down at the book in my hand and seeing the letters in that book, and the letters were glowing. I remember reciting the words as the other apostles were and shortly after, my eyes opened. I believe the Lord was showing me that there is a remnant of apostles that will carry real healing, real power, and possess true authority from the Father. The Holy Spirit explained that He is commissioning a remnant that was the point of the group being "small". Also, note the writing that glowed. The Lord revealed that His word shall be amplified through the mouths of these remnants. The oaths they took were to mean a promise to stand and live by the words of God in order to fulfill His plans on earth.

# NUMBER INTERPRETATIONS

### *Interpretation Inquiry*

*Hey Prophetess Misha. For the last 1-2 years when I look at a digital clock it says 827, cell phone, house phone, computer, etc. I'll notice it on a license plate, on a phone number when it's the first three digits. What's the significance of these numbers together or should I look at them separately?*

God is truly calling your immediate attention. But First, what you want to do is look at them individually. 8 the new beginning, the new thing God is doing in your ministry, I hear God say "New Birthing", birthing something new forth, it's springing forth quickly right now. 2 the number of divisions, but God says, it has been more of a season of separation, and lastly witnessing. The witness means others have noticed your office/calling not only witness but confirming. 7 is the number of completeness and spiritual perfection. I can't help but to see you in a car, and you're pressing on a gas pedal, but then taking your foot off the gas and stepping on the brakes.

When you do this you bring the car to a complete stop. God can't guide a parked car, so keep your foot on the gas peddle in this season so that the Lord may do the new thing. Altogether, these numbers add up to the number 17. Seventeen us victory and perfect completion it's 7 Doubled! God desires to bring your ministry into perfection, he's not done with you keep walking strong and speak out with boldness. These numbers are truly for you prophet, for the ministry God placed within you. It's your season for it to come out because God is bringing you into Fullness. 17 also signifies victory. There are finances, dreams the enemy thinks he's stolen, but God is repaying you divine vindication and recompense

## Her Response:

Hallelujah! Praise God! On target! Bless you, bless you, bless you, Woman of God! Your interpretation matches what He has spoken to me. I will keep my foot on the gas!

### *Numbers Chart[17]*

*10 – Journey, wilderness (Pastor)*
*11 – Transition (Prophet)*
*12 – Government (Apostle)*
*13 – Rebellion*
*14 – Double anointing*
*15 – Reprieve, mercy*
*16 – Established beginnings/Love*
*17 – Election/ Victory*
*25 – Begin ministry training*
*30 – Begin ministry*
*111 – Apostolic/ father/Leaders*
*666 – Full lawlessness*
*888 – Resurrection; Triad affect meaning it will affect three areas of your life*
*10,000 – Maturity*

CHAPTER TEN

# THE GEMATRIA

*"The Gematria is such a powerful tool for biblical interpretation"*

Gematria is a numerological system by which Hebrew letters correspond to numbers. This system, developed by practitioners of Kabbalah (Jewish mysticism), derived from Greek influence and became a tool for interpreting biblical texts. In gematria, each Hebrew letter represents a numerical value. One can then calculate the numerical value of a word by adding together the values of each letter in it. In the realm of biblical interpretation, commentators base an argument on numerological equivalence of words. If a word's numerical value equals that of another word, a commentator might draw a connection between these two words and the verses in which they appear and use this to prove larger conceptual conclusions.

The following HebrewAlphabet Letters along with it's spiritual meaning has been derived from the practitioners of Kabbalah.[12]

## Vav Meaning – 6th Letter of the Hebrew Alphabet

Vav is the power to unite everything that is separated in creation. Literally Vav means hook or peg and the Hebrew letter is a vertical line ו. It represents the Kav, the vertical line extension of the Creator's perfection into the created world, in order to constantly direct it, guiding the cycle of existence step by step, until eventually the perfect Oneness of the Creator which underlies all of creation is revealed. Vav is related to the Orr Yashar, the direct light of the Creator, entering the world.[12]

As the connector, Vav contains the power to connect heaven and earth. It can be considered like a hose, or a tube, which connects and bestows all the energy of the shefa עפש abundance from above down to the created beings. It represents the ladder of Jacob Yaakov – rooted in earth, with its head in the heavens. It is the extension of the essential dot Yod י, which all of creation comes forth from. The Vav can teach us the state of constant presence needed to connect our own heaven and earth (physical and spiritual aspects).[12]

Vav represents the number 6 and represents the six days of the creation of the world, as well as the six physical dimensions (right left, front and back, up and down). The Vav is also representative of the male phallus, the fertilizing agent, bringing life, abundance, continuity, and addition.[12]

## **Lammed Meaning – 12th Letter of the Hebrew Alphabet**

Lammed, the 12th letter of the Hebrew Alphabet is the symbol of learning. It is translated literally as the word for learning and also staff or goad. It is located at the center of the aleph-beith and represents the heart Lev בל; in kabbalah learning is mostly done with the heart and soul, not just the mind. The Lammed indicates that spiritual learning is the heart of human existence. Man's course in life is to learn and express spiritual teachings and practice with every breath of life.[12]

Lammed reaches higher than any of the other Hebrew letters, like a lighthouse high in the air. The shape of the lammed is an undulating movement, and the lammed represents constant organic movement, constant change. Lammed is the lightning strike of energy descending down the two sides of the Tree of Life. Lammed teaches us to learn from everything in life. After one has governed their tendencies in Khaf and no longer has the blockages of the ego interfering, they can begin to learn the spiritual perfection of their own self, and to learn the laws, will, and ways of the Creator. This is the process of learning to align with the will of the Creator.[12]

## Mem Meaning – 13th Letter of the Hebrew Alphabet

The letter Mem is water mayim מים, the waters of wisdom, knowledge, the Torah. Representing both waters and manifestation, it is the ability to dive deep into the wisdom. It is said that in every person is the thirst for the words of the Creator, which are the waters of life. The open mem refers to the revealed aspects of providence, while the closed mem refers to the concealed part of the celestial rule that nonetheless guides us and all of existence. Mem also represents the time necessary for ripening and indicates to us the importance of balanced emotions and of humility.[12]

Mem corresponds to the number 40 and represents the time necessary for the ripening process that leads to fruition. (40 days for the development of the embryo, 40 years in the desert before reaching the holy land, 40 years development before Moses was prepared to be the leader of Israel).[12]

The mem also teaches us about balanced emotions – balancing the watery motions of our feelings. And it is about humility – water is the substance that always runs downhill to the lowest place.[12]

*Figure 1*

## NUN Meaning – 14th Letter of the Hebrew Alphabet

I went to minister at a beloved sister in Christ's ministry and the address to the meeting location just stood out to me. The first time I saw the address on the flyer, it was if the Holy Spirit used a highlighter to amplify the address to me in the spirit! The number 14 is composed of 7+7 which equals 14. 7, of course, we went over this number in the earlier chapter and it means; to make a vow, to swear, to make an oath, completeness, perfection, and wholeness. Nun is the 14th letter of the Hebrew Alphabet and so the 7th of the second letters and repeats the theme of our future or final record.[12] Also meaning inheritance, heaven, day of rest, etc. The Nun emphasis the promised inheritance. The word Nun means fish or continuance as in the continuation or proliferation of "seed". The fish symbolizes in the bible, "A winner of souls".

The letter nun has two forms. The normative nun is bent over (or curves over like it's actually bending downwards) and the final nun is elongated. Both of these forms represent a faithful servant. Faithful in Hebrew is Emun (Strong's Concordance 529) begins with the bent over nun and ends with the elongated nun.

The bent over shape represents a servant in a subservient state, which is a good connotation. God calls Moses a faithful servant. Servant leaders like Moses takes upon the yoke of heaven because the strength of a leader comes from a state of servanthood which is "being humble". A bent over servant who is the strongest of all relates to the number of nun which is the gematria form of 50. 50 is the year of Jubilee, meaning after 7 sabbatical years which is equal to 49 years, is called the year of freedom. It represents a state of redemption but interestingly enough, what happens in the year of Jubilee is that all the indentured servants go free and it's connected to nun all together.

| Hebrew | Name | Sound |
|---|---|---|
| 𐤀 | Aleph | a, e |
| 𐤁 | Beyt | b, bh |
| 𐤂 | Gimel | g |
| 𐤃 | Dalet | d |
| 𐤄 | Hey | h, e |
| 𐤅 | Waw | w, o, u |
| 𐤆 | Zayin | z |
| 𐤇 | Hhet | hh |
| 𐤈 | Tet | t |
| 𐤉 | Yud | y, i |
| 𐤊 | Kaph | k, kh |
| 𐤋 | Lamed | l |
| 𐤌 | Mem | m |
| 𐤍 | Nun | n |
| 𐤎 | Samehh | s |
| 𐤏 | Ayin | ah |
| 𐤐 | Pey | p |
| 𐤑 | Tsade | ts |
| 𐤒 | Quph | q |
| 𐤓 | Resh | r |
| 𐤔 | Shin | sh |
| 𐤕 | Taw | t |
| 𐤘 | Ghayin | gh |

*The Ancient Hebrew Alphabet*[14]

| Pictograph | | Meaning and Interpretation |
|---|---|---|
| 1 | ࡆ | A-Aleph- Ox/strength/leader/father

Apostolic- 1st in command- strong leader. This pictograph relates to the apostolic grace and the apostolic anointing. This meaning points to the leader or father. A father is head of the wife but Christ is the head of the church. |
| 2 | ഗ | B-Beyt House/In- To dwell in. To live in. Psalms 92:13 Those that be planted in the house of the lord shall flourish in the courts of our God. |
| 3 | ✓ | G-Gimel-Foot/camel/pride; The multidude of camels Isaiah 60:6; The multiitude of camels shall cover thee, the dromedaries of Midian and Ephah; all they from Sheba shall come: they shall bring gold and incense; and they shall shew forth the praises of the lord. |

| Pictograph | | Meaning and Interpretation |
|---|---|---|
| 4 | ܕ | D- Dalet - Tent door/pathway year of the open door |
| 5 | ﺡ. | H-Hey- Lo! Behold! The "New Thing" Behold the lord does a new thing |
| 6 | Y | Y-Waw-Nail/peg/add/and this number is the number of man- Elul the 6th Month of the Hebrew calendar counting from Nisan. This month symbolizes a time of repentance. If we look at Romans 5:12, we begin to read cthe contrast of Adam and Christ. It's very clear that Adam sinned and through Adam sin entered the world. Adams sin brought death, so death spread to everyone, for everyone sinned. However, there was a difference between Adam's sin and God's gracious gift. For the sin of this one man, Adam, brought death to many. But even greater is God's wonderful grace and his gift of forgiveness to many through this other man Jesus Christ. This is why you're seeing the number 6 or even |

> 666. 6 is actually the number of man, not the number of evil, the devil, or satan. This false doctrine actually led many to believe this because of what we see in Rev 13:1 Wisdom is needed here. Let the one with understanding solve the meaning of the number of the beast, for it is the number of a man. His number is 666.

Look very closely at this verse in scripture, The bible clearly states that "wisdom is needed here". Let the one with understanding solve the meaning of the number of the beast! Did you catch that?

CHAPTER ELEVEN

# ANATOMY OF DREAMS AND UNDERSTANDING GOD'S VOICE

**Lucid Dreams:** Dreams that are very real in nature even though we know it was just a dream. What does this mean biblically as well as naturally? How can knowing about it help us to better understand our dreams?

Lucid dreaming is the experience of achieving conscious awareness of dreaming while still asleep. Lucid dreams are generally thought to arise from non-lucid dreams in REM sleep.[15]

Lucid dreaming is a dissociated state with aspects of waking and dreaming combined in a way so as to suggest a specific alteration in brain physiology for which we now present preliminary but intriguing evidence. It shows that the unusual combination of hallucinatory dream activity and wake-like reflective awareness and agentive control experienced in lucid dreams is paralleled by significant changes in electrophysiology.[15] Here's an example taken from a sleep journal study of lucid dreams:

## YOU CAN DO THE IMPOSSIBLE!

Normally, when you dream, you're not really aware of what's going on. You can't actively think about things and make your own decisions. It's almost like you're just watching yourself do the actions, but you're not in control. When you have a Lucid Dream however, you become aware of yourself, and the fact that you're dreaming.[16]

You can make decisions, explore and control the dream-world, and pretty much do anything you can imagine. You could fly around the world, meet a celebrity, practice your job interview, or ride around on a giant butterfly; there is no limit.[16]

The reason people are able to have a lucid dreaming experience is that they can 'wake up their minds' and experience things while they're sleeping. Normally when you go to sleep, your brain sort of shuts off and you're not aware of what's going on.

With training and practice, you can unlock the part of your mind responsible for being 'aware' of yourself.[16]

## **BIBLICAL EXAMPLE OF LUCID DREAMS**:

### *Paul's Vision and His Thorn in the Flesh*

*This boasting will do no good, but I must go on. I will reluctantly tell about visions and revelations from the Lord. I was caught up to the third heaven fourteen years ago. Whether I was in my body or out of my body, I don't know—only God knows. Yes, only God knows whether I was in my body or outside my body. But I do know that I was caught up to paradise and heard things so astounding that they cannot be expressed in words, things no human is allowed to tell.*

*2 Corinthians 12:1-4 (NLT)*

I believe that as we dream, our minds are able to enter another dimension or world. Just take a look at the scripture above. We notice that Paul entered into another realm, he was caught up to the third heaven. Lucid dreams can also be a mixture of a dream-trance. When you know you are dreaming, however your mind is conscious of the actual dream in the first place.

Many of the dreams I have, I awake while still dreaming and then I would begin interpreting that dream. Another instance would be as I slept, I woke up next to my husband while still dreaming. I began to explain the previous dream I had to him, then he told me his dream, and I began interpreting that dream.

Many times, my dreams feel so real and often times I am carried over regions and territories. Our spirits become powerful as we connect to Christ Jesus and His word. We can become vessels for Him and begin to hear in the spirit what Jesus hears.

## **DISCERNING GOD'S VOICE IN DREAMS**

The voice of God in our dreams cannot be confused with the enemy's voice. Let's look at some categories of dreams that we can pay close attention to as we begin to interpret our own dreams.

### *Jacob's Ladder*

*As he slept, he dreamed of a stairway that reached from the earth up to heaven. And he saw the angels of God going up and down the stairway. At the top of the stairway stood the Lord, and he said, "I am the Lord, the God of your grandfather Abraham, and the God of your father, Isaac. The ground you are lying on belongs to you. I am giving it to you and your descendants. Your descendants will be as numerous as the dust of the earth! They will spread out in all directions—to the west and the east, to the north and the south. And all the families of the earth will be blessed through you and your descendants. What's more, I am with you, and I will protect you wherever you go. One day I will bring you back to this land. I will not leave you until I have finished giving you everything I have promised you."*

*Genesis 28:12-15 (NLT)*

God's voice is very clear, always directive, and corrective. Both loving and authoritative. It is filled with compassion and compelling truth.

CHAPTER TWELVE

# DREAM DICTIONARY

## ANIMALS

**Alligator/Crocodile**- sea monster. Ancient demonic stronghold that is deeply rooted.; represents a demonic stronghold in the bloodline, possible generational, also any reptilian like creature represents leviathan (see Job 41, Isaiah 27:1). If the alligator's mouth is open it represents anger, aggression.

**Bat-** Represents Witchcraft, fear, soulish.

**Bears of any type**- Ancient demonic spirit, strength, opposition, stronghold.

**Beaver-** Ardent, diligent, clever.

**Black Horse** – feminine; bad times; evil (Rev 6:5).

**Black Panther** – high level witchcraft; demonic activity, or works in darkness.

**Bull-** Anger, aggression.

**Cat**-unclean spirit, self-willed, demonic spirit; friendly cat means your blind to hidden sin; black cat means witchcraft, hidden agendas, a spirit of fear and superstition.

**Chetah**-Swift, fast, spiritual stealth and stamina. On the flip side, could mean danger or a play on words for "Cheater."

**Chicken-** cowardliness; depending on dream tone and setting. Chickens peck when they eat so it could mean pecking at an issue and not getting to the root or pecking at something and not full aware that it needs to be left alone; fault finding.

**Cobras, ratle snake**, - python spirit; seking to squeeze out your prayer life. fear. Mouth open means venom, spiritual attack, or warfare.

**Cow**-substance; provision; prosperity.

**Crab**-spirits of irritation, aggravation and frustration.

**Dinosaur-** Old stronghold, demonic, danger from the past, generational stronghold, spirit of Leviathan in the bloodline.

**Dog-** Unbelievers, hypocrites, friendly dogs could mean disloyalty, friendly dogs; someone befriending you who is possibly unfaithful; be sure to keep in mind the tone of the dream and setting.

**Donkey-** Issachar anointing, gentle strength, stable, on the flip side however, it could mean; stubbornness, hardheaded.

**Dove**-purity, holy spirit.

**Eagle-** soaring to new heights and new levels in the spirit, prophetic accuracy prophetic anointing and calling.

**Elephant-** strength, thick skinned; not easily offended, long preganacy; good stored memory.

**Fish**-souls; people; colored fish denotes people of different nationalities and ethnicities.

**Fox-** Cunning.

**Frog-** hinderance; spirit of lust.

**Goat-** sin, unbelief, stubborn, argumentative, lacking discernment; play on words or "scapegoat."

**Hawk-** unclean spirit; predator, sorcerer; evil spirit; witchcraft; these birds are the opposite of the symbolism of an eagle.

**Hen** – one who gathers; protects.

**Horse** – Power, strength, conquest; spiritual warfare.

**Leopard** – swiftness, sometimes associated with vengeance, predator, or danger.

**Lion** – Jesus "Lion of the tribe of Judah"; royalty, kingship, bravery; confidence; Satan seeking to destroy.

**Lobster** – not easy to approach.

**Mice** – something small that bring destruction; devourer, curse, plague, or timid.

**Mole** – spiritual blindness.

**Monkey** – foolishness; clinging; mischief; dishonesty; or addiction.

**Mountain Lion** – Satan, enemy; predator seeking to destroy.

**Octopus /squid**-Spirits of mind control because of the tentacles that attach to its prey; manipulation, control also, Jezebel. These animals are found in water or deep waters which symbolizes demonic spirits found deeply rooted in the soul- whiuch is the mind, will and emotions, or strongholds.

**Ostrich-** Unclean spirit.

**Owl-** witchcraft, unclean spirit/ can also represent wisdom in the non dream state.

**Ox** – slow change; subsistence.

**Pig** – ignorance; hypocrisy; religious unbelievers, unclean people; selfish, gluttonous; vicious, or vengeful.

**Raccoon** – mischief; night raider; rascal; thief, bandit; deceitful.

**Ram** – sacrifice.

**Rat** – feeds on garbage or impurities; unclean spirit, or invader.

**Raven** – evil, Satan.

**Red Horse** – persecution; anger; danger; opposition (Rev 6:4).

**Sea Gull-**demonic spiritual scavenger.

**Sheep** – the people of God; innocent, vulnerable; humility; submission; sacrifice.

**Skunk** – "stinking up" a situation; unforgiveness, bitterness; or bad attitude.

**Sloth** – slow moving; easy prey, or vulnerable.

**Snake** – Satan & evil spirits (pay attention to the colors and type of snake) deception, lies; Satan; unforgiveness, or bitterness;

**Sparrow** – small value but precious; watched by the Lord.

**Tiger** – danger; powerful minister (both good & evil), soul power, or demonic spirit.

**Tortoise** – slow moving; slow change; steady; old; old way of doing something; wise.

**Turkey** – foolish; clumsy; dumb; thanksgiving.

**Vulture** – spiritual scavenger; unclean spirit; impure; an evil person; greedy; covetous.

**Weasel** – wicked; breaking promises (as in "weaseling out of a deal"); informant or tattletale; traitor.

**Whale** – big impact in the things of the Spirit; deep things of the spirit.

**White Horse** – salvation; rescue; redeem; royalty.

**White Snake** – spirit of religion; occult.

**Wolf** – Agents of Satan and evil; false ministries, false teachers, false prophets, false apostles, false pastors; predatory spirits.

## BODY PARTS

**Arm** – strength; faith.

**Bald Head** – lacking wisdom.

**Beard** – maturity.

**Fingers**[17]
- Thumb – apostolic.

- Pointer – prophetic.
- Middle – evangelistic.
- Ring – pastor.
- Pinky – teaching.

**Hair** – wisdom & anointing.[17]

**Hand** – relationship; healing.[17]

**Immobilized Body Parts** – spiritual hindrance; demonic attack.[17]

**Nakedness** – Positive: being transparent; humility; innocence. Negative: lust; temptation; in or of the flesh.[17]

**Neck** – Positive: support or strength. Negative: stiff necked, or stubborn.[17]

**Nose** – discernment.[17]

**Side** – relationship; or friendship.[17]

**Teeth** – wisdom; comprehension; or understanding.[17]
- Eye Teeth – revelatory understanding.
- Wisdom Teeth – ability to act in wisdom.

**Thigh** – faith.[17]

## CLOTHES

**Bathrobe** – coming out of a place of cleansing.

**Clothing that doesn't fit** – walking in something you're not called to.

**Cultural Clothing** – missionary calling; prayer calling for a particular country or ethnic group.

**Coat** – mantle, anointing.[17]

**Pajamas** – spiritual slumber.

**Shoes** – Gospel of peace.

**Shorts** – a walk or calling that is partially fulfilled.

**Speedo** – to move fast in the spirit.

**Swimwear** – ability to move in the Spirit.

**Tattered Clothing** – mantle or anointing that's not being taken care of.

**Wedding Dress** – covenant; deep relationship.

## COLORS

**Black** – death, or mystery.
- Negative – sin, or darkness.

**Blue** – revelation or communion.
- Negative – depression, sorrow, or anxiety.

**Brown** – compassion, or humility.
- Negative – compromise, or humanism.

**Gold/amber** – purity, glory, or holiness.
- Negative – idolatry, defilement, or licentiousness.

**Gray** – maturity, honor, or wisdom.
- Negative – weakness.

**Green** – growth, prosperity, or conscious.
- Negative – envy, jealousy, or pride.

**Orange** – perseverance.
- Negative – stubbornness.

**Pink** – childlike, or love of God.
- Negative – childishness.

**Purple** – authority, or royalty.
- Negative – false authority

**Red** – wisdom, anointing, & power.
- Negative – anger, or war.

**Silver** – redemption, or grace.
- Negative – legalism.

**White** – righteousness, or holiness.
- Negative – religious spirit.

**Yellow** – hope, or mind.
- Negative – fear, cowards, or intellectual pride.

# DIRECTION

**Back** – Past: (as in backyard or back door). Previous event or experience (good or evil); that which is behind (for example, past sins or the sins of forefathers); unaware, unsuspecting; hidden; memory (Genesis 22:13; Joshua 8:4; Philippians 3:13).

**East** – Beginning (Genesis 11:2); Law (therefore blessed or cursed); birth; first (sun rises in the east bringing hope and new day); false religions (as in "Eastern religions").
- Psalm 103:12 "As far as the east (law) is from the west (grace), so far hath He removed our transgressions from us."

**East Wind** – judgment, hardship (Genesis 41:23, 27; Exodus 10:13).

**Front** – Future or Now: (as in front yard or front porch) prophecy of future events; immediate; current.
- Rev.1:19 "Write the things which thou hast seen, and the things which (presently) are (before, or in front of you), and the things which shall be hereafter."

**Left** – Spiritual: Weakness (of man); God's strength or ability demonstrated through man's weakness; rejected (Judges 3:20-21; Judges 20:16; Matthew 25:33).

**Left Turn** = spiritual change.

**North** – Spiritual: judgment; Heaven or heavenly; spiritual warfare (as in "taking your inheritance") (Deuteronomy 2:3; Proverbs 25:23; Jeremiah 1:13-14).

**Right** – Natural: authority, power; the strength of man (flesh) or the power of God revealed through man; accepted, place of favor (Matthew 5:29-30a; Genesis 48:18; Exodus 15:6; Matthew 25:33; 1 Peter 3:22).

**Right Turn** = natural change.

**South** – Natural: sin; world; temptation; trial; flesh; corruption; deception (Joshua 10:40; Job 37:9).

**West** – End (as in the end of the day); grace; death; last (Exodus 10:19)
- Luke 12:54 "And he said to the people, when you see a cloud (of glory) rise out of the west (grace of God), straightaway ye say, There cometh a shower (blessing); and so it is."

# FOOD

**Apples** – spiritual fruit; temptation; something precious like the apple of God's eyes.

**Bread** – Jesus Christ (as in the "bread of life"); Word of God; source of nourishment; God's provision.

**Grapes** – fruitfulness; success in life; evidence of being connected to Christ (as in John 15).

**Honey** – sweet; strength; wisdom; Spirit of God; the abiding anointing; the sweet Word of our Lord; the best of the land, or abundance.

**Lemons** – sour; a poor sport.

**Manna** – God's miraculous provision; something coming directly from God; glory of God; bread of life.

**Meat** – something meant for the spiritually mature; depth in God's word.

**Milk** – good nourishment; elementary teaching.

**Pears** – long life; pear trees have long life; enduring much without complaining.

**Pumpkin** –Positive: change of the seasons; harvest time; symbol of affection (as in "You are my little pumpkin"); Negative: witchcraft; deception; snare; witch; trick (as in Halloween "trick or treat").

**Strawberries** – goodness, excellence in nature & virtue; healing; sweet & very humble.

**Tomato** – kindness, the heart of God; big hearted; generous.

**Water** – Holy Spirit; refreshing; Word of God; spiritual life.

**Wine** – Positive: working of the Spirit of God; move of God; Negative: drunkenness; love of the world.

## INSECTS

**Ant** – industrious; wise; diligent; prepared for the future; nuisance; stinging or angry words.

**Bee/hornet** – painful; strong demonic attack.

**Butterfly** – freedom; flighty, fragile; temporary glory; transformation.

**Flies** – evil spirits, filth of Satan's kingdom; Beelzebub -"Lord of the flies"; live on dead things; occult.

**Grasshopper** – destruction; drought, or pestilence.

**Moth** – symbol of destruction; deception (as a moth drawn to the flame).

**Roach** – infestation; unclean spirits; hidden sin.

**Scorpion** – evil spirits; evil men; pinch of pain.

**Spider** – occult attack; witchcraft.

**Spider Web** – place of demonic attack; ensnaring, or a trap

## KIND OF DOORS

**Paper Thin doors:** Weakness, tossed and easily blown astray see Eph 4:14 . Tossed to and fro, and carried about with every wind of doctrine.

**Steel Doors**: closed access; restricted access.

**Swing Doors:** Allowing anyone access to your life, to your home. Notice that swing doors do not close and they are always open, therefore, it means vulnerability.

## MISCELLANEOUS:

**Chewing** – thinking on something (as in, "I need to chew on that"), meditating; receiving wisdom & understanding.

**Choking** – hindrance; difficulty in accepting something (as in "the news was hard to swallow"); hatred or anger (as in "I could choke her right now"); unfruitful (as in the weeds growing up and choking the plants).

**Christmas** – gifts; season of rejoicing; spiritual gifts; surprise; good will; benevolence; commercialism.

**Difficulty Chewing** – hard saying; difficulty receiving something.

**Flying** – call or ability of move in the higher things of God; understanding the spirit realm of God.

**Kiss** – coming into agreement; covenant; seductive process; enticement; deception, betrayal; betrayal from a trusted friend.

**Life seasons** – may include former places you have been/lived, and/or former schools, tests, jobs, etc.
- Reflect on the significance of that season.

**Miscarriage** – losing something at the preparatory stage, whether good or bad; plans aborted .

**Pregnancy** – in process of reproducing; preparatory stage; promise of God; Word of God as seed; prophetic word; desire, anticipation, expectancy; purposes of God preparing to come forth
.

**Repeating activities** – God establishing a matter or issue; repeating because you are not listening
.

**Running** – faith; perseverance; working out one's salvation; moving forward with purpose.

**Swimming** – living in the Spirit; moving in the things of the Spirit; operating in the gifts of the Spirit.

## MODES OF TRANSPORTATION

**Chariot:** powerful encounter with the Holy Spirit.

**Fast sporty vehicles (mustangs,challengers..etc):** represents a fast moving ministry powered by the Spirit.

**Ship, steamboat:** large ministry; if the ship is not moving, the ministry may be large however, it is not moving, and it denotes a lack of the Holy Spirit and the Spirit of God cannot flow through that ministry; complacency, or stagnation.

**Steam ship Line:** (Very Large Boat that carries containers filled with Goods). This symbolizes one who is skilled at trading goods or services, commerce; especially of foreign countries. It also symbolizes someone who is sent to the marketplace.

**SUV**: large mobile ministry.

## OBJECTS

**Cell phones, telephones, Television:** represents communication with God, communicating with heaven; could also symbolize the flesh.

**Check** – favor.

**Credit Card** – presumption; lack of trust; attempting to walk in something that you don't have yet; debt.

**Crown** – symbol of authority, to reign; seal of power; Jesus Christ; honor, reward.

**Doors:** symbolize entry points; both legal access and illegal access.
- Doors that do not fit on the hinges; represents trying to fit your ways or your process of doing something instead of trusting God's process and his ways.

**Dream setting:** dark/night time; represents a struggle, trial, trouble, or hidden sin.

**Gate** – spiritual authority; entrance point for good or evil.

**Fruited Trees** – healing.

**Key** – spiritual authority; wisdom; understanding; ability; Jesus.

**Ladder** – ascending or descending; promotion or demotion; going higher into the things of God; portal of heavenly activity (as in Jacobs ladder had angels ascending and descending).

**Microphone** – influence; ministry; authority; being heard.

**Microwave** – impatience; quick work; convenient; sudden.

**Mirror** – God's Word; a person's heart; vanity.

**Money** – gain or loss of favor; power; provision; wealth; spiritual riches; authority; strength of man; covetousness; greed.

**Security Alarms:** secure in the spiritual realms, alertness, protection; guarding.

**Television** – spiritual sight & understanding; entertainment; fleshly cravings & desires; fleshly spirit; love of the world.

**Trees** – leaders; mature believers; steady.

**Roses:** This is a symbol of romance, relationship, deep intimacy or bond; negative; seduction, or seducing/enticing.

# PEOPLE

**Baby** – new ministry or responsibility that has recently been birthed; new beginning; new idea; dependent, helpless; innocent; sin.

**Bride** – Christ's church; covenant, or relationship.

**Carpenter** – Jesus; someone who makes or mends things; building something spiritually or naturally; preacher.

**Giant** – Positive: godly men (as in "a giant of the faith"); strong; conquer; Negative: demons; or defilement (as in the Philistine Giant Goliath).

**Harlot / Prostitute** – a tempting situation; appealing to your flesh; worldly desire; a demon; spirit of lust; spiritual apostasy.

**Hijacker** – enemy wanting to take control of you or a situation.

**Husband** – Jesus Christ; actual person.

**Lawyer** – Positive: Jesus Christ, our advocate; mediator; Negative: Satan, the accuser of the brethren; legalism.

**Mob** – false accusation.

**Policemen** – authority for good or evil; protector; spiritual authority.

**Prisoner** – a lost soul.

**Shepherd** – Jesus Christ; pastor, leader (good or bad); selfless person; protector.

**Twins** – Positive: double blessing or anointing; Negative: double trouble.

## ROOMS IN A HOUSE OR BUILDING

**Attic** – mind, thought; history; past issues; family history; spiritual realm.

**Basement** – hidden; forgotten; hidden issues; foundation; basics.

**Bathroom** – spiritual cleansing; prayer of repentance; confession of sins to another person.

**Bathroom in full view** – humbling season; others aware of cleansing; transparency.

**Bedroom** – intimacy; rest; privacy; peace; covenant (as in marriage).

**Dining Room/Eating** – partaking of spiritual food; fellowship.

**Kitchen** – heart (as in the "kitchen is the heart of the home"); spiritual preparation; going deep in the Word; spiritual food & feasting.

**Restaurant kitchen** – teaching ministry; greater influence or impact; preparing to serve people the Word.

## ROOMS/BUILDINGS/AND PLACES

**Atrium** – light & growth from heaven.

**Auditorium/Theatre**-A place of of performance, prophetic arts, spiritual rhythm and flow with in the holy spirit gathering.

**Auto Repair Shop** – ministry restoration, renewal & repair.

**Back porch-** The former things of the past or history.

**Barn/warehouse** – a place of provision & storage.

**Bedroom/bed-** A place of rest, sleep, paralysis or stagnation, or resting on issues that need to be addressed.

**Buying, or living in, the house of a known person in the ministry** – God has a similar call on your life.

**Castle** – authority, fortress, or royal residence.

**Country General Store** – provision; basics, or staples.

**Elevator-** shifting position in the spirit; going up means to ascend in the spirit or go into higher spiritual realms. Going down in the elevator denotes depression, feeling down, trial/trouble depending on what's happening in the dream could mean demotion.

**Front Porch-** Vision of the future, or future events that will take place.

**Garage** – place to rest & refresh; place of protection; or covering for ministries or people.

**Garden** – a person's heart; love; intimacy; growth.

**Gas Station** – receiving power; refilling or "refueling" of the Spirit; empowering.

**Hallways**- spiritual and natural Transition.

**Hotel** – transition; temporary; place to relax or receive.[17]

**Jail / Prison** – bondage; rebellion; addiction.[17]

**Kitchen**- A place or season of preparation.

**Library** – learning; knowledge; research.

**Living room**-Learning, gathering of brethren.

**Mall** – market place; provision for all your needs in 1 place; Negative – self centeredness; materialism.[17]

**Mobile Home / Trailer House** – temporary place, condition or relationship; movement, easily movable; poverty.[17]

**Mountain** – place of encountering God; obstacle; difficulty; challenge; Kingdom, or nation.[17]

**Office building** – getting things accomplished; productivity.

**Park** – rest, peace; leisure; God's blessing; vagrancy.[17]

**Previous / Old Home** – past; inheritance; memory; revisiting old issues.

**Prisoners** – lost souls; persecuted saints.[17]

**Restaurant**-A ministry of service/helps; serving spiritual food.

**Roof** – spiritual covering.[17]

**School-** A place or season of learning the spiritual things; being taught about something or someone; teaching ministry, or teaching anointing.

**Shack-** Poverty mindset; famine; lack; shortage; bankrupt; debt.

**Stadium:** A ministry of tremendous impact.

**Stage**-A place of display and god bringing thing to the center of attention; on display; depending on the dreamer, could mean fleshy/soulish/vain.

**Staircases**- Heavenly portals or dimensions in the spirit. going up; ascending into heaven, greater heights access, authority/rank,promotion. down: demotion, backsliding, failure, rebellion. Play on words: steps that need to be taken.

**Swimming pool**- a place of spiritual refreshing; god's spirit; immersed in the spirit of god, represents the prophetic, the spirit of prophecy and being immersed in the spirit of prophecy.

**Tent** – temporary place of rest; meeting place with God.

**Theater** – on display, visible; going to be shown something; clarity; spiritual sight; fleshly lust.

**Two-story House** – double anointing.[17]


**Windows** – vision; letting light in, spiritual sight, or opportunity (as in an "open window of opportunity").

**Zoo** – strange; chaos; commotion; very busy place; noisy strife.[17].

## TRANSPORTATION

**Airplane** – (size & type of plane correlates to the interpretation) prophetic ministry; going to heights in the Spirit; new & higher understanding.

**Armored Car** – protection of God.

**Automobile** – personal ministry or job.

**Bicycle** – individual ministry or calling requiring perseverance.

**Bus** – church or ministry.

**Chariot** – major spiritual encounter.

**Coal Car** – on track; being directed by the Lord.

**Convertible** – open heaven in your personal ministry or job.

**Fire Truck** – rescue; putting out fires of destruction.

**Fred Flintstone Car** – human effort.

**Hang glider** – going somewhere in the Spirit; driven by the wind of the spirit.

**Helicopter** – mobile, flexible, or able to get in Spirit quickly.

**Limousine**:
- Positive: being taken to your destiny in style;
- Negative: materialism.

**Mickey Mouse Car** – purpose is colorful & entertaining.

**Mini Van** – family.

**Motorcycle** – fast; powerful; maneuverable.

**Moving Van** – transition; change.

**Ocean Liner** – impacting large numbers of people.

**Riverboat** – slow, but impacting many people.

**Rollercoaster:**
- Positive: a wild ride that God is directing, exciting, but temporary;

- Negative: a path of destruction that first appears exciting; an emotional trying time with ups and downs.

**Sailboats** – powered by wind of the Spirit.

**Semi-truck** – transporting great quantity of goods

**Spaceship** – to the outer limits, or spiritually speaking.

**Speedboat** – fast, exciting, or power in the Spirit.

**Submarine** – undercover and active, but not seen by many; a behind the scenes ministry, or hidden ministry.

**Subway** – undercover and active, but not seen by many; a behind the scenes ministry, or hidden ministry.

**Stagecoach** – rough, difficult ride; old way of doing something (good or bad).

**Taxi Cab** – a shepherd or hireling for someone (driving); paying the price to get where you are going (passenger).

**Tow Truck** – ministry of helps; gathering the wounded.

**Tractor** – slow power; may speak about a need to plow.

**Train** – a movement of God; denomination.
**Truck** – ability to transport or deliver.

**Tugboat** – providing assistance; ministry of helps.

## WEAPONS

**Arrow:**
- Negative: accusation from the enemy.
- Positive: blessing of children; focus; specific message (as in "shooting an arrow with your life").

**Dart** – curses; demonic attack; accuracy.

**Gun** – spiritual authority good or bad; spiritual attack.

**Knife** – brutal attack or gossip; protection (if you are holding it).

**Shield** – faith; protection; God's truth; faith in God.

**Sword** – Word of God; far-reaching; authority.

# WEATHER

**Dirty Snow** – impure.

**Earthquake** – upheaval; change (by crisis); God's judgment, disaster; trauma, shaking; shock.

**Fog** – clouded issues or thoughts; uncertainty; confusion; temporary.

**Hail** – judgment; destruction; bombardment.

**Ice/Ice Storm** – hard saying; slippery; dangerous.

**Rain** – blessing; cleansing (clear rain); trouble from enemy (dirty rain).

**Snow** – blessing; refreshing; righteousness; purity; grace (Isaiah 55:10-11a).

**Snow Blizzard** – inability to see; storm that blinds you or obstructs your vision.

**Snow Drift** – barrier; hindrance; opposition.

**Storms** – disturbance; change; spiritual warfare; judgment; sudden calamity or destruction; turbulent times; trial; opposition.

**Tornadoes** – destruction, danger; judgment; drastic change; winds of change (negative or positive depending on the color of the tornadoes).

**White Storm** – God's power; revival, outpouring of the Holy Spirit.

**Wind** – change (as in "winds of change are blowing");
- Positive: Holy Spirit.
- Negative: adversity.

## ABOUT THE AUTHOR

Misha Wesley has an established School called M.M.O.C which is a Theological School of Prophetic Arts and Worship. The goal of M.M.O.C is to raise up and equip the five fold and dreamers that have strategic accuracy in the realm of visions, dreams and numbers to impact their cities, states, regions and nations. Misha Wesley has an apostolic international call to mobilize a guild of prophetic dreamers, visionaries and awaken, train and release them for the effective work of ministry.

Her training will help you not only to interpret your dreams, but to pray strategically over your communities, regions and territories. It is not for those who think they know it all but those who are truly hungry to seek a change by the use of strategic prayer over your marriages, equip your children with prophetic tools, pray over your place of employment and understand how dreams provide direction, correction and instruction in the area of your business and finances. She gives an understanding on numbers and its language to bring out a greater depth of scripture, for people's life and their community! She is also the author of "The Heart Of A Young Prophet."

# REFERENCE

1. H2492 - chalam - Strong's Hebrew Lexicon (RSV). Retrieved from https://www.blueletterbible.org//lang/lexicon/lexicon.cfm?Strongs=h2492&t=rsv
2. G3677 - onar - Strong's Greek Lexicon (KJV). Retrieved from https://www.blueletterbible.org//lang/lexicon/lexicon.cfm?Strongs=g3677&t=kjv
3. Derivation. (n.d.). Retrieved March 30, 2018, from https://www.merriam-webster.com/dictionary/derivation
4. H2451 - chokmah - Strong's Hebrew Lexicon (KJV). Retrieved from https://www.blueletterbible.org//lang/lexicon/lexicon.cfm?Strongs=H02451&t=KJV
5. Wisdom. (1998). In Strong's exhaustive concordance: New American standard Bible. (Updated ed.). Retrieved from http://biblehub.com/hebrew/2452.htm
6. Mastin, L. (2010). Memory Consolidation. Retrieved from http://www.human-memory.net/processes_consolidation.html
7. Oliwenstein, L. (2009, February 25). Caltech Scientists Find Evidence for Precise Communication Across Brain Areas During Sleep. Retrieved from http://www.caltech.edu/news/caltech-scientists-

find-evidence-precise-communication-across-brain-areas-during-sleep-1510
8. Bladh, W. (2016, October 16). Sleep Paralysis. Retrieved from https://www.webmd.com/sleep-disorders/guide/sleep-paralysis#1
9. schizophrenia. (2018). Online Etymology Dictonary. Retrieved from https://www.etymonline.com/word/schizophrenia
10. Schizophrenia. (n.d.). Retrieved March 30, 2018, from https://www.merriam-webster.com/dictionary/schizophrenia
11. Moed. (1998). In Strong's exhaustive concordance: New American standard Bible. (Updated ed.). Retrieved from http://biblehub.com/hebrew/4150.htm
12. Spiritual Meanings of the Hebrew Alphabet Letters. (n.d.). Retrieved March 31, 2018, from http://www.walkingkabbalah.com/hebrew-alphabet-letter-meanings/
13. Figure 1. Nun. (n.d.). Retrieved March 31, 2018 from http://www.sofer.co.uk/html/nun_to_samech.html
14. The Ancient Hebrew Alphabet. Adapted from Learn the Ancient Pictographic Hebrew Script by J. Benner (n.d.). Retrieved from http://www.ancient-hebrew.org/learn_ancient.html
15. Voss, U., Holzmann, R., Tuin, I., & Hobson, J. A. (2009). Lucid Dreaming: A State of Conscious-

ness with Features of Both Waking and Non-Lucid Dreaming. Sleep, 32(9), 1191–1200.
16. What Is Lucid Dreaming? A Beginners Overview. (n.d.). Retrieved April 7, 2018, from http://howtolucid.com/lucid-dreaming-definition/
17. Ibojie, J., Jackson, P. J., Goll, J and M., Wolverton, S., Milligan, I. (2018). Biblical Dream Dictionary. Retrieved April 7, 2018, from http://www.unlockingyourdreams.org/dream-dictionary/

# INDEX

## A

ability, 7, 11, 61, 75–76, 79, 84, 87, 98
accuracy, 98
anointing, 41, 75–76, 78, 80, 89
Ant, 82
apostles, 39, 50–55, 57
apostolic theologians, 52–53
authority, 47, 55, 77, 79, 86–87, 89, 91, 98

## B

believers, 24, 32–33
betrayal, 84
bible, 30, 32, 34, 39, 63, 67
bitterness, 73
bread, 42, 80–81
breakdown, 30, 33

## C

Calling dreams, 3, 19
captives, 49
cherubims, 41, 50
chokmah, 11–12, 102

consistency, 11
covenant, 46–47, 76, 84, 88, 90
creation, 40–41, 50, 59–60
creator, 24, 59, 61

D

danger, 69–71, 73, 100
Daniel, 48–49, 53
Daniel's prayer, 48
darkness, 36, 48, 69, 77
death, 51, 54, 77, 80
defilement, 77, 88
deliverance, 24–25
demonic attack, 75, 82, 98
demons, 24, 88
demotion, 20, 87, 91, 94
depression, 77, 91
destruction, 71, 82, 95, 97, 99–100
direction, 9, 17, 21, 50, 78, 101
discernment, 10–12, 71, 75
disciples, 11, 42, 46
divisions, 37, 56
dominions, 41, 50
DREAM DICTIONARY, 68
dreamer, 2, 4, 17, 94, 101
dreams, 2–6, 8, 13, 16–22, 25, 28, 32, 48, 54, 56, 70, 86, 91, 101

E

earth, 36, 38, 40–42, 44, 46, 50–51, 55, 59
emotions, 4, 23–25, 30, 72
enemy, 2–4, 16, 56, 72, 98–99
evil, 69, 72–74, 78, 82, 86, 89
evil spirits, 73, 82
Ezekiel, 36, 41, 49–50

F

faith, 18, 20, 37, 46, 74–75, 84, 98
father, 9, 37, 43, 46, 48, 55
fish, 42–43, 63
flesh, 5, 45, 47, 75, 79–80, 86, 88
foolishness, 71

G

gematria, 58
gifting, 32
gifts, 6–9, 20, 42, 48, 83, 85
glory, 6, 15, 41, 43, 46, 77, 80–81
grace, 9, 42–43, 78, 80, 99

H

heart, 2, 4–5, 15, 45, 47, 60, 81, 90
heavens, 36, 38, 43, 49, 54, 59, 63, 79, 86, 90, 94

Hebrew letters, 58–60
highways, 16
holiness, 77–78
Holy Spirit, 14, 17, 21, 38, 42, 44–45, 54–55, 62, 81, 85, 100
humility, 61–62, 73, 75, 77

I

ignorance, 41, 72
interpretation, 13–14, 16, 18–19, 25, 35, 45, 49–50, 65–66, 95

J

Jesus, 3, 7–8, 39–40, 42–43, 46, 51, 54, 71, 87–88
judgment, 10, 79, 99–100

K

Kabbalah, 58–59
kingdom, 39, 51, 53, 93
knowledge, 7–8, 10–11, 34, 47–48, 61, 92

L

leader, 61, 63, 87, 89
light, 36–37, 41, 48, 54, 90, 94
Lord's wisdom, 4

lust, 70, 75, **88**, 94

## M

maturity, 53, 57, 74, 77
memories, 22–25, 28, 78, 93
ministry, 6, 33, 45, 56–57, 85, 87, 91–93, 95, 97–98, 101
miracles, 42–43
Moses, 61, 63
motives, 10–11
mourning, 15
movement, 41–42, 92, 98
multiplication, 38, 42–43

## N

numbers, 5–6, 14, 25, 32–33, 35–52, 55–56, 58, 60–63, 67, 101

## O

operation, 9–11, 32–33, 47
opposition, 68, 73, 99

## P

pastor, 54, 57, 75, 89
peace, 17, 76, 90, 93

perfection, 44–45, 51, 56, 62
perseverance, 77, 84, 95
prayer, 3, 45, 76, 89
prayer life, 69
promises, 15, 55, 84
prophecy, 47, 79, 94
prophetic ministry, 44, 95
prophetic word, 21, 49, 84
prophets, 8–9, 52–54, 56–57
protection, 87, 92, 95, 98
provision, 43, 69, 80, 87, 91–92

R

REAL PEOPLE, 13
rebellion, 57, 92, 94
revelatory, 7, 32–33, 47
ROOMS, 89
royalty, 71, 74, 77

S

sacrifice, 72–73
Satan, 3, 71–74, 89
schizophrenia, 30, 103
seasons, 15, 19, 41–42, 48, 56, 81, 83–84, 92–93
sins, 77–78, 80, 88, 90
sleep paralysis, 29, 103
SLEEP STAGES, 27, 29–30

sorrow, 14–15, 77
stairs, 18, 20
strength, 63, 68, 71, 74–75, 79–80, 87
symbolism, 71

T

temptation, 75, 80
transitions, 4, 14, 29, 57, 92, 96

U

union, 37, 39

V

victory, 56–57
visions, 4–6, 8, 13–14, 17, 20, 22, 25, 28, 94, 99, 101
voices, 8–10, 17
vow, 44, 62

W

warning dreams, 3, 16
waters, 7, 36, 38, 61–62, 72, 81
WEAPONS, 98
WEATHER, 99
Whale, 74

whispers, 5, 28
wilderness, 43, 57
Wine, 81
wisdom, 9–12, 48, 61, 72, 74–75, 77–78, 80, 83, 87, 102
witchcraft, 69, 71, 81–82
witnessing, 38, 51, 53, 56
Wolf, 74
Worship, 101

Z

Zion, 15
Zoo, 94

www.ingramcontent.com/pod-product-compliance
Lightning Source LLC
Chambersburg PA
CBHW071521080526
44588CB00011B/1520